I WAS ALBERT SCHWEITZER'S SECRET MISTRESS

POETRY AND STORY

BY JUDY LIESE

BLUE LIGHT PRESS ◆ 1ST WORLD PUBLISHING

1st WORLD
PUBLISHING

SAN FRANCISCO ◆ FAIRFIELD ◆ DELHI

I WAS ALBERT SCHWEITZER'S SECRET MISTRESS

Copyright © 2015 by Judy Liese

1ST WORLD LIBRARY
PO Box 2211
Fairfield, Iowa 52556
www.1stworldpublishing.com

BLUE LIGHT PRESS
www.bluelightpress.com
Email: bluelightpress@aol.com

BOOK & COVER DESIGN
Melanie Gendron

COVER ART
Gary Liese

AUTHOR PHOTOGRAPH
Gary Liese

FIRST EDITION

Library of Congress Control Number: 2014921208

ISBN 9781421886954

I WANT TO THANK:

My teacher, mentor, and friend, Diane Frank for showing me how to coax a poem into its best existence.

My workshop peers for their encouragement and suggestions.

My husband, Gary, for his unfailing support and for his gorgeous cover painting.

Diane and Erik, and my friend, Janet, for their careful proofreading.

All my family and friends who have acknowledged my poetry offerings over the years and who keep asking, "When is your book coming out?"

Melanie Gendron, who put it all together.

All my teachers, especially Miss Brooks and Mr. Sager.

Our Mini-Aussie, Fargo, who takes me on those amazing walks.

ACKNOWLEDGMENTS

Grateful acknowledgment to the following magazines and anthologies in which some of these poems were previously published:

Eclipsed Moon Coins, Lyrical Iowa, Circle of Stones: From the Blue Light Press Summer Workshop; Nine Voices and a Saxophone: Poems from the Blue Light Press Summer Workshop, Mermaid Dreams: From the Blue Light Press Summer Workshop; and Embroidered Horizons. "The White Dog" was previously published as a chapbook.

Shortly after I met Joyce Uhlir in Diane Frank's on-line poetry workshop, we discovered that we had both attended school in Milwaukee, Wisconsin at the same time over forty years ago. She was getting a master's degree at the university while I was in nursing school, just a few blocks away. Both of us literally spent all our free time walking along beautiful Lake Shore Drive along Lake Michigan. We must have passed each other hundreds of times without ever meeting! When we finally met in person, it was as if we had known each other all our lives. I was devastated when she lost her battle with cancer in 2011, but I could feel her spirit looking over my shoulder through every phase of putting this book together. So, this book is:

FOR JOYCE

TABLE OF CONTENTS

LITTLE JUDY

ALASKA

MARRIED LIFE

LIFE IN CALIFORNIA

DOG DAYS

IN MEMORIUM

LITTLE JUDY

I WAS ALBERT SCHWEITZER'S SECRET MISTRESS

They say that your first love changes you forever.
My husband and I haven't been getting along lately.
I wonder if he suspects that I have been
your on-and-off mistress for thirty-five years?

Sweet sixteen and you hadn't kissed me yet.
I thought maybe you were waiting
until I was ready.
So I hung your picture, flanked
by the tattered pages of a Bach prelude
over my desk and prepared myself
for medicine, religion, philosophy,
theology, and music.

Going through nursing school
drew lines of exhaustion on my face.
My eyes began to reflect an emptiness of spirit.
My feet ached from walking
those endless corridors of pain.
I had chosen a harsh school,
harsh as the most savage jungle,
good preparation for our life together, I thought.

Becoming Lutheran was easier
because I already was one.
But I had to struggle with philosophy and theology,
leaping over huge chasms of nothingness with Kierkegaard,
supported only by invisible parachutes
clinging to our backs like the emperor's new clothes —
peering out of Plato's cave, struggling in vain
to see beyond the shadows.

1

I begged my piano teacher to let me play Bach,
which she said I had no ear for.
I played it anyway.
You were my teacher,
the only one to cognize the sensuality of Bach.
After hearing you play, I could hear
that sensuality, like the touch of velvet on my cheek,
in the playing of others.

I remember sitting in the choir loft
during a Bach prelude and fugue.
I felt your fingers tickle my earlobes.
The upper melody stroked my hair,
brushed against my face.
My lips tingled.
The contrapuntal notes
filled my hollow head with your burning scent.
Those low pedal notes marched up and down my spine,
stirred a visceral response that shocked me.

After nursing school I stood before you in my white dress,
my bride's cap decorated with a black ribbon instead of a veil,
my wedding shoes — white oxfords.
But you rejected me at the altar.
I was unsuitable, you said; my fatal flaw —
blond hair, blue eyes, and pale, delicate skin.

Today in the middle
of a sticky Iowa summer,
sweat runs down my back,
drips off the tips of my hair.
I feel I will die before fall finally comes.
Your harsh rejection
looks more like a kindness now.

I've learned to hear my own voices,
and you did tell me that your quest
could never be anyone else's.

This morning you spoke to me.
You said that you saw a snowflake
land on your coat sleeve.
You watched it melt
into the fabric of your coat.
You said that for a few moments
you were that snowflake.

I feel myself
sink into the silver strands
of your dead hair,
melt into the bone
at the top of your skull,
float in the dark space
behind the empty sockets,
reach out a soft fingertip
to touch your delicate spine.

BABY IN A BOX

While war rages in Europe
and Japan attacks Pearl Harbor,
a baby in a box struggles for life,
fighting for each painful breath
in a green hospital room at Saint Elizabeth's.
The doctor says she probably won't live.

"We'll try the new sulfa drugs,
but she'll need absolute quiet.
Keep the parents out of the room
and don't pick her up.
Just leave her alone so she can rest."

The baby sees a world of shadows,
window shades drawn against the light.
Rustling black skirts of the nuns
mingle with whispered prayers
that can't satisfy the longing,
memory of soft arms holding, rocking
a soft voice singing.

She recognizes the silhouette of her daddy
framed by the open door and calls for him
in the only way she knows.
But her frenzied cries bring the nuns
who firmly close the door,
leaving her alone once again.
As her frantic gasping for air eases,
she feels her body float up
out of the box to hover near the ceiling
for a moment before passing through walls
to a small chapel where three nuns light candles

sending fragrant prayers upward
for the recovery of the baby
they are not allowed to hold.

The baby slips inside the prayer,
feels gentle arms around her,
listens to a low and lovely singing,
a suggestion of wings,
soft breath on her cheeks,
knowing that she will one day
cradle her own baby.

SNOWFLAKES FALLING ON MY HEART

I grip snow-sodden mittens in baby teeth,
cupped, chapped hands held out
to capture lacy white flakes, no two alike.

I hold winter's treasures close to my face,
but the ice crystals melt into my palm
before I can see the design.

I tug wet mittens over red hands
and lift my face, stick out my tongue,
sweet-tasting touches of cold.

When Mom sings to me at night, the music brushes
the tips of my ears three times,
Winken, Blinken, and Nod.

The snow falls in big clumps now.
I sway a little in the cold air,
smell clean whiteness like freshly ironed sheets,
feel angel kisses on my cheek.

KAUKAUNA ROAD

When I am two, we live in Kaukauna.
The tall radio off the bedroom I share with my sister
plays Grofe's *Grand Canyon Suite*
and . . . "Call for Philip Morr . . . iss!"
just before I fall asleep.
Or "People Are Funny," my mother laughing
with the people in the radio.

I remember Mother hanging up the clothes,
wearing her old brown coat with the big wooden buttons,
singing under her breath,
making the wooden clothespins perch like birds.
Sometimes, Mom makes clothespin dolls for me
with eyes, nose, and mouth drawn in pencil
and a little ruffled skirt
she gathers from her scrap bag.
I am making one of them dance on the front step
when Ralphie comes over to play.

"Let's run away," he says,
reaching out a chubby arm.
A long red road winds up over the hill
where the sun sleeps.
I take his hand and we toddle off
toward the top of the hill
where I have never been.
We walk and walk and finally at the top
I can see more red clay road, houses and trees
and an endless sky
filled with gray clouds and excitement.

"You come back here right now!"
Ralphie's mother races up the hill breathing hard,
her face red and angry.
She grabs his chubby arm,
and drags him down the hill,
smacking his bottom with her other hand
all the way to his house.

I am frozen with fear.
My own mother is walking up the hill,
slowly because she has a bad heart.
She takes my hand, walks back down the hill,
matching my little steps with her own.

"You mustn't ever go in the road.
It's too dangerous," is all she says,
and I never do.

But after we move to Milwaukee,
I dream about red clay roads.

MOTHER'S WOODEN BUTTONS

My tiny two-year-old hand
barely covers the enormous wooden buttons
that hold my mother's brown tweed coat together,
a shield against the frigid Wisconsin wind
that whistles over the hill,
and slips icy fingers under our coats.

I like the smell of those buttons,
like the wooden clothespins
she uses to fasten wet sheets
to the clothesline in our back yard,
the wind lifting them
to the cold blue sky,
sheets swiftly turning stiff
in the freezing air.

I see my little yellow dress
standing by itself as if made of cardboard.
But I am not even in it!
This strange sight sends a shiver through me.
I clutch the bottom of my mother's coat
and press my face against
the smooth wooden buttons,
breathing in the familiar smell,
comforted by the way
my mother's coat keeps out
the icy winds of change.

PICKERAL LAKE

I can't swim. Too little to be left alone,
I squat at the end of a long wooden pier
where the leaky rowboat bobbles at the end
of a thick, slightly slimy rope.

Nearby, Dad sits on the edge,
pant legs rolled up,
bare feet in the water,
unknotting my tangled fishing line
for the umpteenth time.

I peer into murky green,
try to see a turtle
or maybe a cloud of polliwogs
becoming fat frogs.
Abra Kadabra Ali Kazam!

Did I just see something shiny
way down at the bottom?
Pirate's Gold!
Ker-Splash!
Eyes open wide,
I see a whole different world,
all greeny-brown and seaweed
like flowers poking up out of the sand.
Tiny minnows tickle my toes.
Clams scattered here and there lie half open.
Something inside peeks out.

Toward the middle of Pickeral Lake,
a mermaid flits among the shadows, calls my name.
I see my skinny arms and legs,
strands of hair floating, transformed and green.
Is this what dying is like?
Strong arms pluck me out of the water.
"Are you all right?"
Dad pounds my back,
but I never breathed in any water
because I hadn't completely turned into a fish.

WILD HAIR

I hate my hair,
the rag-curls I have to sleep on,
the little nests of snarls,
the pinpricks of pain on my scalp
as Mom yanks the comb through,
all the while insisting it doesn't hurt!

One summer day, Mom hacks off my hair.
Washing this new short haircut
takes a minute instead of half an hour,
and combing doesn't hurt anymore.
Yippee!

When Mom isn't looking,
I go outside and spin around,
arms outstretched, bare feet
dancing on the cool grass.
The wind lifts my hair.
The sun warms my scalp.
I run. I twirl. I jump.

Mom calls me in,
furious that I didn't sit still,
that I ruined her comb-out.
She lifts me up to the big mirror
in her bedroom, so I can see
how terrible I look now.

I see me, flushed and happy, eyes shining.
Fine strands fly away from my face
like an escaping halo,
wild and free.

THE GIFT

I remember the handkerchiefs, edged with Belgian lace,
I bought for my mom out of my allowance,
set aside because she had plenty of hankies;
the pink flowered scarf I gave her for Mother's Day,
tucked away in the bottom dresser drawer
because it didn't go with anything.
When I was in senior high school,
I saved up my babysitting money
to buy her a silver, filigreed music box
that played "Laura" in tinkling notes like summer rain.
Every day on my way home from school
I looked in the window of Spector's Jewelry Store,
and it was still there when I finally had
the seventeen dollars and fifty cents,
just days before my mother's birthday.
It went up on the top shelf
of the built-in, floor-to-ceiling china cabinet,
because who in the world would get a music box
for someone who was losing her hearing.
She never even turned the key.

I thought she couldn't love me,
but now another memory drizzles down
through the cloud of years.
My mother sang to me —
Winken, Blinken, and Nod at night,
Marble Halls by day,
and O Holy Night at Christmas.
I knew those songs were just for me,
because I could feel her pure voice
lift a thousand veils
to let me see the timid love
that hid behind her bitter mouth.

LOBSTER

My eight-year-old eyes
stare in horror at these wonderful creatures,
handcuffed in their watery prison,
behind unyielding glass.
barely able to move around
in the cloudy, crowded waters.

I could smash the glass,
sending water everywhere.
While the screaming people
scramble to climb up
on red checkered tabletops,
I could stuff the lobsters
in my pink, princess purse
and smuggle them home
where I would cut their cruel wires
and hide them in our bathtub
until I could carry them in a pillowcase
down to the Fox River
and let them go.

Or I could order a toasted cheese sandwich
and pretend the lobsters are really enchanted princes
who will turn back at the last minute and tell the chef,

"How would you like to be tossed
into a big pot of boiling water?"

SAWDUST

I race the first two blocks to Jacob's Meat Market.
Red maples with rough bark whir past in a blur.
If I bring back the correct change,
Mom will give me a nickel.
At City Park I stop to catch my breath
and make sure the folded-up dollar
is still in my sticky fist.
I turn toward the hand I write with,
count out two more blocks and there it is.

A little bell rings when I open the door.
I can smell fresh wood from the sawdust
rolling under the thin soles of my red tennis shoes
as I shuffle to the glass case.
The man behind the counter knows me.
"How may I help you today, young lady?"
I tell him, "Half a pound of summer sausage cut thick."

He makes adjustments on the machine,
grabs a fat sausage from the case in his meaty hand,
plunks it on the metal plate.
He turns the crank and perfect rounds fall
in an overlapping pattern on a square of white paper.
which he puts on a scale.
I heard Mom's canasta friends say
they thought Mr. Jacobs put his thumb
on the scale to make it weigh more,
but I don't see any thumb.
He catches me staring at him and I decide
to study the sawdust under my feet.

He places the summer sausage on brown butcher paper,
folds it over, and fastens the end with tape.
I hand him my damp dollar
and he opens the cash register — ping!
He empties the coins into my outstretched hand.
I hesitate, but have to ask.
"Is that the correct change?"
His face flushes dark red.
"Of course it is."

All at once, I become aware
of another smell underneath the sawdust.
Something sickening.
I grab the package and run out the door
past the park, past the maple trees.
I run all the way home.

Mom says I've brought back the correct change,
so she gives me my nickel,
says I can go to the corner store
for candy if I want to,
but I feed my piggy bank instead.

INTERIORS

The summer I turn ten,
Mom and Dad decide I am old enough
to stay with my Aunt Hulda and Uncle Paul
on their Door County farm.
I am so excited that first night,
but fall into sleep in the small upstairs bedroom
that was mine for the summer,
at the first sound of frogs singing.

In the middle of the night,
my skin tingles into wakefulness
for no reason at all.
A luminous Mickey Mouse tells me it's two a.m.

I jump out of bed, flopping belly-down
in front of the open window.
From here, I can see clear across to the barn.
There, fastened by its back legs
to the top of the open barn door
hangs a lifeless Holstein.
Light illuminates the inside of the barn.
Someone's truck headlights spotlight the carcass.
Every detail stands out so sharp,
as if I am looking through magical glasses.

Uncle Paul and some other men
move shadow-like in front of the barn.
Pieces of conversation float up.

"When did she get hit?"
"Hope we didn't wait too long."

With one sweeping gesture, the insides are exposed,
which are not flat and next to each other,
but around and behind, or in front.
The anatomy chart in our old encyclopedia
never prepared me for all this roundness,
the way the curves fit together.

The glistening viscera hangs there for a moment
before dropping into the vat,
leaving behind a dark hollow.
When they unwrap the outer covering,
I spot a familiar configuration
in the black-and-white pattern.
So it's Daisy. I swallow hard and look away.

But then I see the muscles under the skin.
They don't resemble the stuff you see in butcher shops.
Here, each curved line represents some precise movement.
These beautiful swirls converge at strategic places,
producing an economy of design which reminds me
of something out of my deepest dreams.
The men work quickly to divide the rest
into manageable parts,
then load them onto the truck.

I look hard that night,
through the clear air,
deep into the interior of Daisy, the cow,
but I never do see that place
where her life once resided.

PAL

Uncle Paul doesn't like me to pet the dog
because of his bad back leg.

"If you accidentally bump that leg,
he'll bite you real bad.
It won't matter that he likes you."

But I am careful
to stay away from the back legs,
the bushy thumping tail.
I stroke the cream-colored fur
on top of his head where it merges
into the rough darker coat on his back.
I feel prickles of thistle and burr
through the thick matted pelt,
inhale the rich doggy smell.

Aunt Hulda calls me for lunch.
Getting up, I lose my balance,
falling against the leg.
I hear a throaty snarl
and look up in time to see close up,
the open jaws, lips pulled back,
the sharp white teeth.
But, with great effort,
Pal wrenches sideways,
snaps the empty air.

WATER AND FOG

Part One: Door County, 1949

At first, I don't want to drink
from the metal cup hanging
on a chain attached to the pump.
Everyone drinks here, even the people
who come to pick cherries.
But Uncle Paul just laughs,
says the sun will kill any germs.

That first sip, so cold and sweet,
slides down my throat,
creating icy sparks that tingle
all the way down to my toes,
and a delicious metallic taste
they say is from iron in well water.

Part Two: Sonoma, 2009

After a year,
I discover we have an artesian well
and we stop buying bottled water.
This morning, cold tap water fills my glass,
a recycled almond butter jar from Trader Joe's.
I toss a handful of blood pressure pills
toward the back of my throat and drink,
chilled taste of stone.

From my deck, I watch Pacific fog
tumble over the Sonoma mountains
on the other side of the valley

rolling over the space between us,
enveloping my outstretched arms,
open mouth, and wild morning hair,
until I feel the pounding surf and taste the salty sea.

FOUR KINDS OF EXHILARATION

I fall off the pier
into a watery world
apart from parents,
hanging suspended
in a green seaweedy
kind of heaven.

I ride carousel horses
up and down, around,
the outside world a blur,
Mom and Dad,
a smear of color.

At my riding lesson,
the retired racehorse pricks up his ears
at the sound of a distant gunshot,
takes off across the dusty autumn field.
We float over brown grass,
my hands wrapped in his tangled mane,
legs snug around his belly.

My new friends whisper
that Leon's pretty wild,
but I go with him anyway in his little MG,
to the back roads behind Anchorage,
racing over a hundred miles an hour with the top down,
my hair slapping flushed cheeks,
mouth open in a feral smile,
tasting distant icy glaciers,
the lure of northern lights.

What happened to that girl?
When did I learn to be so cautious?
How can the petals of a California Poppy
close up at night once they feel
the light from galaxies on their skin?

BEAUTY HAS HARD EDGES

I feel sorry for Miss Grundy,
straight, mouse gray hair
carefully waved, printing precise letters
on the green blackboard.
I sense movement behind me,
Ping! A spitball hits
the teacher in the back of the neck.

"Who did that?" in a high quavery voice.

Miss Grundy doesn't like children.
Neither do I, here in junior high
where the desks are too small,
the boys rough and rowdy,
no longer my pals.

I turn around and shake my head,
Mouth the words, "Stop that."
But Steve's wide blue eyes
shine with unconcealed delight.
His beautiful lips compress into a smirk.

Miss Grundy turns back to her slow printing.
I wish the class wasn't so mean.
I feel his hand down the back of my blouse,
then, a ferocious stinging, like red ants.
Letting out an involuntary yelp, I jump up,
clawing at my back.

"Miss Grundy, Steve Jolin put
itching powder down my neck!"

She turns around, thin lips a straight line.
"Miss Klingbile, go out in the hall at once!
Steve wouldn't do a thing like that.
Steve is a good boy."

FALLING IN LOVE WITH MR. SAGER

Pulling gently on the silken threads,
he lures me out of my cocoon,
slowly uncovering what lies trembling.
Wet sticky wings held close.

Five days a week I attach
myself to my assigned desk,
peek through one of the pinholes
observing as he draws out
a reluctant tough kid,
expelled from two other classrooms,
for belligerence, Mr. Sager's
Social Studies period five
his last chance.

"Mr. Kruger, Wisconsin is thinking
of lowering the age for drinking beer
from twenty-one to eighteen.
How do you think this would change things?"

Jack shifts uneasily in the undersized desk.
We are all holding our breath, waiting.
A long silence, then he blurts out,
"Hell, nothing would change at all.
Eighteen-year-olds are already drinking beer."

When the laughter dies down,
Mr. Sager looks at Jack,
who is looking at the floor.
"Class, Mr. Kruger's opinion
is just as valuable as yours.
Maybe he understands
the world better than we do."

Jack looks up, grins, "Yeah."

I am astonished.
Even boys like Jack are safe in this room.
I never learn to speak up in class,
but I do on paper. I chew up words,
spin them into story.

And when I get my creations back,
Mr. Sager has written words
like "excellent" and "very perceptive."
He tells us you don't have to fall
in love to get married,
that he could have been happily married
to any one of a dozen women.
A collective gasp at such heresy,
but I am comforted.

On my very last day of school,
I sit in Mr. Sager's class.
When I feel his hand on my shoulder
I shudder all the way down to my toes
but inside, where it can't be seen.
He hands me my final paper.
I hold it in both hands,
staring without seeing.
Slowly the words,
scribbled in green ink
come into focus.

"A+ You're quite a sprite."

Something cracks open.
I step out on tiny twig feet,
spread wet wings,
glide all the way home.

THE HARLEY

Eric carries cigarettes
in the rolled-up sleeve of his white T-shirt
and rides a Harley Davidson to high school.
I think he looks like James Dean in *Rebel Without a Cause*.

He was a loner until Deanna
stopped hanging out with the popular girls.
Now we see her hitching up her skirt,
to climb on the back of Eric's motorcycle.
They clatter and roar out of the parking lot,
her bright red hair flying behind.
The other girls stare after them,
lips parted, conversation halted for a moment,
until the two are out of sight.
What they say then, I don't know.

I imagine my mother,
corners of her mouth drawn down
wondering out loud, *what kind of parents
allow such reckless behavior?*

Being on the fringe, I never know
what the other girls whisper about,
but I think maybe this good girl
could reform the bad boy
and they would live happily ever after.

At night I dream of riding on the back of a Harley Davidson,
wild hair flying, heart open and unafraid.

A CRACK IN THE WALL

I like the faded yellow roses
with gray-green leaves,
embellishing my bedroom walls
in our house on Franklin Street,
a fixer-upper, held together
by square nails and century-old wallpaper.
But, Dad wants to see what's underneath.

We moisten the walls with boiling water
from Mother's steaming tea kettle,
peel off many layers,
the pungent smell of musty plaster filling my head
even after I am sitting at my desk in school.
When the walls are finally dry,
the bare surface reveals a million little cracks.
I am allowed to paint the bumpy walls
with lilac-colored paint I pick out myself,
making the tiny room truly my own.

At night, the dim glow from streetlights
brings out forms in the uneven plaster
that look like a donkey with long ears
stepping down from a hill onto a road,
a very pregnant Mary on his back.
Off to the side, holding the bridle,
a bearded Joseph leads the way.
Do they have to stay there all night,
trapped inside the wall?
I fall asleep staring at their shifting forms
and with the morning light, they disappear.

One night I wake up from a dream
to see the wall crack open from floor to ceiling.
From that narrow opening, a shadow donkey
places one hoof gingerly onto the wooden floor.
He enters my room, followed by a shadow Joseph
who urges the donkey forward in a soft whisper.
They hurry past my bed,
through the glass of the Eastern window.

TWO SNOWY THANKSGIVINGS

1. Door County, Wisconsin

Mom and Dad would never ask
our nineteen-forties Ford
to carry us through the snow,
but we don't see any snow when we
start out, heading north on Highway 41,
only heavy gray skies and a hard cold
the heater can't seem to dent.

As we leave the Door County State Forest
and venture into rocky farmland,
clumps of white magic fall from the sky.

"Over the river and through the woods"
we sing for the umpteenth time
as we pull slowly into Grandpa's farm
and park our black, snow-spattered car
among a scattering of venerable trucks,
wearing white hair and beards.

Inside, I see laughing faces,
red from the heat of the woodstove,
the old oak table groaning with platters of turkey,
mashed potatoes, ham, and green beans,
apple pies cooling on the windowsills,
chocolate cake with a thick layer of frosting.

I don't remember how we got home.

2. Milwaukee, Wisconsin

Tension I am too young to understand,
hovers over our kitchen table.
Mom got up at five a.m. to roast the turkey,
but already delicate flakes of snow
drift slowly outside the window
and Dad wants to cancel our trip to Aunt Hattie's.

We make it as far as Fond du Lac
before Dad pulls up to a train station,
the snow flying sideways past the windshield.

We're going to take a train to Milwaukee!
I've never been on a train before.
Inside I am singing, but I'm wise enough
to keep my excitement to myself.

After the train begins to lurch down the track,
I steal a glance at Mother, sitting across the aisle,
looking straight ahead, mouth a determined line,
the turkey sitting in a blue enamel pan on her lap.

More fun to look out the window
where snow and speed smudge trees,
streetlights, houses,
and obscure the milky sky.

FINDING MY PLACE

I sit cross-legged in our gravel driveway,
holding a clay-colored stone with black markings,
a nice addition for my collection.
Inside, the chirps and squawks of Mom's canasta club
sift through the window screens,
like starlings fighting over sunflower seeds.
Lillian, from across the street, swears and pounds the table,
screaming at her partner for holding back a vital ten.
Shocked silence slowly turns into normal conversation.
Hum of honeybees.

Mom's voice floats above the chatter.
"No, Judy didn't get my singing voice . . . tone deaf . . .
can't seem to follow the melody with the rest of us."

My stone falls back into the gravel, forgotten.
This can't be true — I love to sing!
I run to Buffy, my cocker spaniel,
cry into her tawny fur.
She licks the tears off my face,
but she doesn't say my mother is wrong.

That fall, I join the sixth grade band,
choose the French horn because I like its curly shape.
I even get to play in a real concert
to a scattering of moms and one dad — mine!

In late winter I slip on black ice,
knock out my two front teeth on the curb.
The dentist tells my parents no more band,
so I have to turn in my curly horn.

I find myself in the alto section of the school chorus
because they had too many sopranos.
The harried director takes time to assure me
they'll find a place for me if I can't sing harmony,
but I easily follow the alto line,
feel the chords through the soles of my feet.
I'm not tone deaf after all. I'm just an alto!

KINDNESS

Dad's new Jewish colleague shyly admits he's homesick.
Few Jews choose to live in Appleton, Wisconsin.
Mother smoothes her blue cotton housedress, frowns.
Next day she brings home a cookbook from the library,
sits at our white painted kitchen table
and reads, as the Milwaukee Braves baseball game
floats from the radio.

That weekend Mom packs two picnics,
a regular one in our big straw basket with the folding lid
and a smaller one that looks suspiciously
like my old Easter basket, the contents wrapped
in a clean dish towel Mom has embroidered
with yellow daisies.
The little one is for Mr. Weinburg, she says,
and is filled with kosher pickles, Jewish rye bread
and special hot dogs from Jacob's Meat Market.
That's the first of many family outings with Mr. Weinberg.

Toward the end of summer, we all go to the carnival.
I'm not allowed to eat anything because carnivals are dirty,
but they let me ride the carousel and the Ferris wheel.
Sweaty, exhilarated, and a little dizzy,
I stop in front of the cotton candy booth,
to gaze longingly at spun-sugar pink perfection.
Mom catches my eye and frowns, shakes her head.
I know I won't get the just-a-lot-of-air,
waste-of-money and you-won't-like-it lecture
with Mr. Weinberg standing right there,
but I turn away from the temptation.

I see Mr. Weinberg look at me intently for a moment.
Then he strides over to the booth,
orders a large cotton candy, and holds it out.
"For me?" I whisper, and he nods his head, winking at me.
I glance at Mother, but I see she's decided to be polite.
I thank him before closing my eyes,
opening my mouth wide for that first bite of heaven.

It's like biting into a cloud at sunset,
the forbidden fruit in the Garden of Eden.
Sixty years later, I can still taste that sweetness.

MY EIGHTH BIRTHDAY

All I want is a plane ride,
but Mom says no, never, forget it.
I won't settle for anything else.

Mother's no means NO, so I am amazed
to find myself being driven to the airport,
me in the backseat scarcely daring to breathe,
afraid Dad will turn our Studebaker around
in the middle of College Avenue to go back home.

We stand around a tiny plane with an open cockpit,
the only one available,
and to everyone but me, too dangerous!
After much discussion, I am finally allowed to go
if my sister agrees to go with me.

Jean, squished between me and the pilot,
is not happy when I hang over the side
to watch the shrinking landscape.
Cars turn into ants crawling along Highway 41,
houses become playing pieces in our Monopoly game.

Jean's warnings to be careful fade into the background.
The steady hum of the engine seeps through my skin,
vibrates behind my eyes, shaking loose
a deep knowledge that I and my world
have been forever transformed,
like the Fox River below,
a thin strand of greenish ribbon.

AFTER KAFKA

Mom, sitting on the porch steps,
blows a puff of smoke at a buzzing mosquito,
then turns toward our neighbor.

"She's at that awkward stage, all arms and legs."
As if I am not right there, perched on the railing.
I go in the house and shut the door. Hard.
But her voice drifts through the open window,
    " . . . look like sticks."

The next morning, I awaken early.
A patch of sunlight inches
across the wooden floor.
I fling back the pink sheets
to find my limbs in a tangle.
All eight of them!

I put one translucent white leg
on the floor and then another,
the bottom of my feet tacky,
as if I could climb walls.

Not easy, coordinating all those extremities,
but I find myself at the bottom of the stairs,
sliding the dead bolt, turning the doorknob,
pushing the screen door open.

I lift my spider face to the sun,
glistening and iridescent.
The town is deserted now,
but soon everyone will see this long-legged beauty
sauntering down the streets of Appleton,
and run screaming from the strangeness of it all.

CLIMBING THE PLUM TREE

Mom looks at me crossly. She is hanging wet sheets in our backyard. I've just asked her what lies beyond the edge of the universe. "If you keep thinking about crazy questions that have no answers, you'll end up in the back ward of a lunatic asylum! Go read your comic books."

I turn quickly so she won't see the tears stinging my eyes, run to the plum tree in the corner of the garden and climb up to my sitting branch. Below me, I see bees humming around the raspberry bushes, collecting sweetness to spin into honey. Next to the raspberries, rows of green beans, carrots, and tomatoes wear fat fruit, the colors of sunset. Reaching up, I grab a deep purple plum, warm and scented from the sun. When I bite into it, sticky juice trickles down my chin, drips onto my yellow striped T-shirt.

If I put the seed in a flowerpot with dirt and water, magic will release a shiny green sprout that grows into a big tree like the one I'm sitting in. I stare at the sticky pit in the palm of my hand, peer past the pulpy remains, through the rough wall into the dark mysterious center, where something smaller than the tiniest thing I can imagine lies coiled and ready to wake up.

LIKE HEIDI

When I was a child, I wanted to be Heidi
and live on a mountain, close to clouds.
My best friend would be a boy
who takes care of sheep.
If I only had a mountain home,
I too could be strong like Heidi,
standing up to her grandfather
when he acted mean.

Sixty years later I have my mountain home.
There are no sheep on this mountainside,
but Fargo, our Mini Aussie, herds invisible flocks
in the field of wild grasses in front of our house.

Sometimes I can feel Heidi's ghost
looking out from my eyes,
listening through my ears.
She teaches me to appreciate
the way fog layers the hills,
how sunlight changes colors of green.

We love to watch
the glittering waters of the bay,
and as evening closes in,
the flickering lights of Sonoma.
Later, the soft *whoo-whoo* of owls,
the occasional whinny of horses
float in the silence of night.

ALASKA

THE GLACIER

The glacier moves
its pale, blue-green bulk
imperceptibly over the frozen land,
only to break apart,
falling into the deep
aquamarine water at its base,
dissolving into itself.

LEAVING HOME

At the airport, Mom pushes me away,
angry, when I try to give her a hug.
"If you're really going to go, just leave."
Stunned, I realize they think I won't do it.
I turn and march toward the portable stairs
and board the plane.

Wisconsin farmlands, squares
of brown and green, recede.
Soon I can't see the red barns.
Highways, looking like spilled
sewing threads, gradually disappear.
No one wants me to go to Alaska,
but I dream of northern lights,
mountains with clean jagged peaks.

I try not to think about living at home,
my old bedroom, filled with child furniture
and stuffed animals, familiar and safe.
By night, Charge Nurse in Intensive Care.
By day, my parent's youngest child.
I feel my heart, thumpa, thumpa
in time with the drone of the engine.

As the plane floats into Anchorage,
I feel amazed and light.
A yellow taxi takes me to the hotel
through a night so black
I can scarcely tell the difference
between the lights of the city
and a sky teeming with bright stars.

THE WHITE DOG

Mr. Fitch, the personnel director of the psychiatric hospital, pulled on his tie and pressed his lips into a frown when I told him I had no car.

"You'll need one in Alaska," he said, "and they should have told you that before you moved all the way up here."

"I took a taxi from the hotel in town," I said, wanting to sound more grown up than I felt. "Actually, I've been here for several days now, you know, getting used to the place."

Mr. Fitch leaned back in his chair and tapped his pencil on the oversized oak desk. "Then you've had time to find an apartment."

"Well, no."

"Judy, don't you know that apartments are at a premium out here? You should have . . . " Mr. Fitch sighed, closing his eyes for a moment. Then he picked up the phone and pushed a button.

"Hello, Janet. Tell them I'll be gone for a couple of hours. Yes, I'll be back by lunch."

Pulling keys out of his pocket, Mr. Fitch stood up. He finally smiled. "Get your coat. We're going house hunting."

The apartment complex, more like a two-story motel, nestled in a wooded area less than a mile from the hospital.

"You'll be able to walk to work during the two week orientation, but once you start working the graveyard shift, you will have to get a car." Mr. Fitch waited for me to reply.

"Don't worry," I said, smiling. I didn't have the heart to tell him that two months' rent plus a hundred dollars for the damage deposit had wiped out my savings. Back in 1962, $250 represented nearly a month's salary for an RN just out of nursing school. Here in Anchorage, my rent would be half a month's gross pay. Thank goodness the meals would be free.

My first day off, I bundled up and went outside to explore my new surroundings.

"Howdy, neighbor!"

I looked up to see a middle-aged man in his shirtsleeves, cleaning the windows of his black Chevy.

"Hello." I said. I hadn't met many people who lived there, and I couldn't think of anything to say.

"Whatcha gonna wear when it gets cold?"

I looked down at the full-length green wool coat my mother picked out for me, remembering how she rejected my hug at the airport, pushing me away saying, "Just go then, if you're really going to go!" The look of disbelief on her face when I actually picked up my suitcase and walked toward the plane was etched somewhere in the front of my brain where it floated into my awareness at odd times. When I looked up, I noticed the huge grin on my neighbor's face, the crinkly lines around his eyes. I decided to ignore him, so I walked through the parking lot to the highway and never looked back.

When I got to the highway, I stopped for a moment, not knowing where I wanted to go. My new mailing address, Star Route B, sounded very romantic, but strange. I felt as though I had moved to the edge of a distant galaxy. For a moment, I wished I was back at the hotel where I had easy access to the library, souvenir shops, and even a J.C. Penny store. Then I noticed the snow-capped mountains at the end of the road and my sense of isolation lifted. As I walked toward those inviting peaks, a mounting sense of excitement replaced any loneliness I might have felt. Within five minutes, a red truck pulled up and stopped next to me.

"Hi there, need a lift?"

"No, thank you. I'm just out for a walk."

"I see. Where are you headed?"

"Those mountains." I said, pointing with one mittened hand.

Laughing heartily, the man drove off. Two hours later I knew why. The mountains were no closer than when I had started. Now I was laughing at myself as I turned around to head back home. Clearly I had a lot to learn about my new home.

Without the mountains, the land looked mousey. Even the stubby pines displayed a dusty pallor as if they were thirsty. Above the horizon, thin gray clouds did not yet hold snow, although the air carried the scent of snow.

Halfway back, I heard a rustling sound behind me and turned to find not a wolf or a moose, but a large white dog. When he trotted over, I pulled off a mitten and let him sniff my hand with his cold, wet nose. When the plumed tail began to move slowly back and forth, I stroked the fresh, clean fur. I swear

I could feel some kind of electric energy coming off the tips of his hair. Then he bounded off, but instead of disappearing into the woods, he accompanied me back home, weaving in and out of the trees along side the road. When I got to the apartment, I turned to say good-bye, but the white dog had vanished. After that, he came with me on all my walks, seeming to appear out of nowhere. In my mind, I called him "Lightning."

As I got to know my neighbors better, they told me the Chugach Mountains were over thirty miles away, but no one knew anything about a white dog. "Don't ever touch a sled dog," they warned, as if anyone could resist that snow-scented fur.

As the weeks passed, I settled into my strange new life, overcoming my initial terror at work after discovering I would be supervising nurses twice my age with years of experience in the field of psychiatric nursing. They were from Canada while my nursing license came from Wisconsin. My inexperience turned out to be an advantage, though. When the progressive hospital administrator announced there would be no fences, no locked doors and no restraints, the older nurses were horrified, but I felt right at home with this innovative approach. New psychiatric drugs were just coming into use. I didn't realize that Thorazine was just another kind of restraint.

For the first time, I was actually dating. Lots of guys. Then, just one, a handsome Nordic type who worked days in another part of the hospital. Eddie knew all the fun places around Anchorage. After he got off work, he took me bowling in town or ice skating on Goose Lake. One time we drove to the Mendenthal Glacier in his friend's old Chevy. We stood there, holding hands, as the whole face of that massive wall broke loose and plunged into the pale aqua water below, dissolving into itself. That night, he told me what it was like to be a born-again Christian and revealed that he was studying to be a Baptist minister. I found this fascinating. We Lutherans considered such talk to be in poor taste, but Eddie made it all sound so natural, gently drawing me out, encouraging me to talk about my own religious beliefs.

"You were right not to believe that unbaptized babies burn in hell," he said. "And I want you to know that your Pastor Wilhelm was wrong to tell you such an evil thing." Eddie forgot his gloves on my couch when he left that night. When I held them up to my nose, I could smell leather, but they also smelled like Eddie. I lay awake for hours that night, inhaling the scent of his Sterling cologne.

At first, he only let me see his charming side, so I tried to ignore his temper and his unreasonable jealousy. Once David, a friend from work, gave me a ride home from the grocery store. When Eddie came over for supper that night, his eyes looked icy and the blue veins at his temples pulsed with fury.

"I see what you do when you think I'm not looking! I know you talked to David in the store today. I saw him drive you home. I don't want you talking to that creep. Do you understand me?"

I felt bewildered. "Well, come in and get something to eat. The meatloaf is getting cold."

His fury left as quickly as it had come. "It's just that I love you so much," he grinned, and I felt flattered.

We never actually talked about getting married. Somehow, it was just understood. Just before Christmas, I transferred from the tiny Lutheran church down the road to the Baptist church in town. They persuaded me to play the organ for them, and I found myself spending long hours practicing the Christmas music. So maybe I was just tired that night when Eddie took me house hunting. When we got back to my apartment, he complained about my lack of enthusiasm for the project.

"I thought you would be more excited about planning our life together." His eyes iced over in that now-familiar coldness. I didn't dare tell him I didn't want to move out of what was mine into what was his. So, I must admit I was in a funny mood when I walked to work that night.

It was during the two-week orientation, when I went to work during the daylight hours, that I discovered the shortcut. A narrow dirt road wound around through the woods for half a mile and came out at the parking lot in back of the hospital. I never felt afraid to walk alone. Tonight a full moon reflected off the silvery snow, lighting my way better than the flashlight I carried in my coat pocket. I loved every inch of this path. Hoping to catch a glimpse of the northern lights, I decided to leave the path, wading through the snow to the middle of a large clearing. I thought it might be easier to spot those shifting green columns of light that spread across the horizon and leaped up to touch the top of the night sky. But, when I looked up, I saw something quite different.

A shower of ice crystals floated down, surreal in their slowness, like floating flakes in a really expensive snow globe. They winked on and off as they caught edges of moonlight on their delicate, polished surfaces. I don't know how long I stood there, but when I looked down again, my mind felt clear as the night, scrubbed clean by cold Arctic air. I felt as though I understood everything - the earth and my place in it. Reluctantly, I started to leave, but I couldn't find the place where I crashed through the brush. After circling the clearing twice, I knew I was lost. In the distance, I spotted a light, and somebody was awake, somebody who could tell me how to get back to the road. Bare bushes pulled at my woolen coat as I approached the tiny log cabin. The light from the windows seemed friendly and I didn't hesitate to knock on the door. A few seconds later, it swung open. An old lady stood framed in the doorway, her white hair pulled back in a bun. Unlike the other old ladies I knew, she was dressed in blue jeans and a green sweatshirt with a brown gingham cat appliquéd on the front.

"Do I know you?" she asked, peering into the darkness. Behind her, a large white dog got up from his blanket in front of a wood-burning stove and trotted over, tail wagging.

"You don't know me, but I know your dog." I smiled in what I hoped was a reassuring way. "And I'm afraid I'm lost."

"What's the matter with me?" she said. "You must be freezing. Come on in."

I stepped inside and closed the door.

"You must take off your coat and get thawed out," she said, and taking my coat, disappeared into a back room. The white dog stood there, pushing his cold nose into my hand. I patted his head, but my attention was drawn to a desk in the far corner of the room. It held a small, funny-looking television set, white with rounded corners, and what looked like little heaters on either side. Instead of a picture, the screen glowed with an eerie light and I saw typed words. Just then, the old lady came back. When she caught me staring, she hurried over and pushed a button on the television. The strange light flashed off. Then she turned off the desk lamp, throwing that end of the room into a shadowed darkness.

"Come and sit down. Have some tea. You must tell me how you came to be lost and how in the world you know my dog."

As we sat at her kitchen table, sipping hot peppermint tea, I answered her questions. She laughed when I told her about the mysterious white dog who seemed to have a sixth sense about my walking habits.

"I wondered where he went. Sometimes he's gone for hours."

"He's a great walking companion," I said, gulping down the last of the fragrant tea. "I don't know his real name. I've been calling him Lightning."

"Lightning is a wonderful name." she said, "Sometimes when I brush him at night, I turn out all the lights just so I can watch the sparks jump out of his fur."

I knew I should leave, but the heat of the stove and the clean scent of burning wood lulled me into a kind of drowsy complacency. In some fuzzy way I was aware of mugs being refilled. She was asking me something.

"I'm sorry, what did you say?"

"I was asking you about your job over at the psych hospital. Do you really like that kind of work? Did you always want to be a nurse?"

I felt confused. "My high school counselor asked me if I wanted to be a teacher or a nurse, so I thought what the heck, I'll be a nurse, and here I am." I waited for her to laugh, but she just stared at me, her eyes magnified behind those round glasses.

"Everybody has to have a job and this is a good one. I guess I like it well enough." Why was I feeling so defensive? Finally, she leaned back in her chair and sighed. "You know, I just realized that I don't know what to call you. I'm Mrs. Washington."

"Sorry, I should have introduced myself right away. I'm Judy Miller."

Well, Judy Miller, tell me what you absolutely love to do. What are you passionate about?"

I thought for a minute. "I love to read and walk in the woods. I love classical music and writing poetry." Uh-oh, I didn't mean to say that last part. No one wants to hear that you write poetry.

But Mrs. Washington clapped her hands in delight. "I'm a writer too! You must bring me some of your poems. I would love to read them."

I felt my face flush. "I haven't written anything here. Besides, I only write for myself."

She smiled, but I could see that behind her eyes, she was laughing at me. "Why bother writing a poem if you're not going to share it with others?"

"I'm sorry," I stammered, "you've been very kind, but I really must get back to work."

"Of course, you do. Let me get your coat. Forgive an old woman for keeping you so long. Sometimes it gets a little lonely out here."

Once I got my coat on, she showed me out the back door and pointed to a birdhouse mounted on a tall pole at the edge of the trees. "There's a footpath just to the right of the birdhouse that will take you back to the old road."

I turned to go, but her hand on my shoulder held me back. "Just remember one thing," she said. "Don't give up the things you love just to do what other people expect you to do."

When I got to the birdhouse, I looked back. She stood on the back porch, her silver hair luminous in the moonlight. I followed the path and soon found myself on the road again, just five minutes from the hospital. To my amazement, I was not late for work.

That morning, as soon as I got home from work, I wrote this poem about my experience in the woods.

ALASKA

The moon, round and smiling,
sprinkles frost crystals
onto my upturned face.
"Wake up!" she sings.

Stars chant childhood hymns,
revealing what the inside looks like
without boundaries,
the night sky,
an upside-down cradle.

With unexpected clarity,
I perceive the friendliness of pine.
Arms filled with snow,
they tell me why
the aurora borealis
paints heaven into being.

Eddie showed up just as I was writing the last word. I had forgotten that we were going out for breakfast. He spotted my poem on the desk and snatched it up. As he read it, I could see his veins, throbbing at the temples, a familiar sight, and a bad one.

"I don't want you writing this garbage!" he shouted. I tried to show you how to listen to the Lord, but these are the words of the Devil!" After tearing the paper into tiny pieces, he opened the door and threw the confetti into the wind, where it swirled across the parking lot and disappeared into the woods.

"Now we'll just forget about this and have a nice breakfast." Eddie was all smiles and charm now.

I stared at this stranger who was acting as if nothing had happened. "I don't think we should see each other any more."

"What's that supposed to mean? We're getting married you know."

"I don't think so, Eddie. Sometimes, I'm afraid of you." For the first time, I sensed the violence coiled behind those blue eyes.

"You should be afraid of me!" he screamed as he went out the door, slamming it behind him. Seconds later, I heard the squeal of tires.

Two nights later I was getting ready for our Wednesday night typing class at the Anchorage Community College. I wondered if he would show up in the old Chevy as usual, or if I would have to drop the class. Maybe we could patch things up.

He showed up all right — with his new girlfriend in the front seat. I crawled into the back seat and tried not to notice how they held hands and giggled, whispering, instead of talking.

After they brought me home, Eddie called out, "See you next Wednesday."

The next day, I took the bus into town and bought my first car, a little red and white Hillman Sunbeam.

Now, forty years later, I relax in my favorite chair, holding the letter that opened this flood of memories, the letter from Alaska offering me a writing grant. This includes the use of a log cabin for one year, rent free, to write a collection of poems using images of the great Alaska earthquake of 1964. Although the cabin is a bit primitive, they assure me it has electricity and will come equipped with a new desktop computer, complete with satellite dish. They saved the best news for the end.

"Of course, your dog is welcome, but you will have to pay the airfare for any companion, canine or otherwise."

This makes me smile. I bought my Akita about a year ago, right after my husband died of a sudden heart attack. The big goofy puppy grew into a beautiful good-natured dog, and I would hate to leave him behind.

"Here Lightning, come here, boy." The big white dog trots up, pushing his cold wet nose into my hand.

"Good boy! Guess what? You and I are going to Alaska!"

ALASKA SNAPSHOT

The photograph, lost long ago,
now lives in my heart, unyellowed by age,
memory falling back in time.

In my family, nice young girls
don't travel alone to this wild new state
to work as a psychiatric nurse.
After that first night in my tiny apartment,
tossing, turning in blankets of doubt,
I devour a Milky Way and a glass of water,
bundle up in my green plaid coat,
grab my Brownie camera
and open the door on a world
transformed by frozen fog.

White branches lift glittering arms
to dazzle a milky blue sky.
Diamonds in the grass,
along Star Route B, light my way,
as I snap picture after fairy tale picture,
saving the last for a simple white church on a hill,
steeple piercing heaven itself,
blessing my new life.

ALASKA PSYCHIATRIC: SPRING, 1964

He's standing in a corner on the periphery,
as I reassure the other refugees from Valdez,
their group home annihilated after the Alaska earthquake.
Through a tangle of anxious voices, I make my way
across the dayroom to reach him.
Faded blue striped overalls match faded blue eyes.
He has no teeth, giving his face a caved-in look.
A thatch of yellow hair sticks up
like a rooster's cockscomb.

"GO AWAY!" His voice harsh, startles me.

"Hi, I'm Judy. What's your name?"

"GO AWAY!" Louder this time.

"Are you hungry? Lunch is ready."

"GO AWAY! GO AWAY!"

I ask one of the caretakers from Valdez about him.

"Oh, you mean David.
Those are the only words he heard, growing up,
the only ones he knows.
He doesn't really want you to go away."

My heart does a flip-flop.

"Hey David," I say softly, "Let's go eat, OK?"

"Go away," he answers politely,
then shuffles beside me to the dining room,
his big hand folded gently around my own.

NEW YEAR'S EVE PARTY AT THE ANCHORAGE BAPTIST CHURCH

Eddie says I'm not sociable.
OK, I'll be sociable!

I am drawn to the brown eyes,
beneath an Air Force buzz cut,
earnest behind coke-bottle glasses.
He is insisting his name
should have been Todd, not Gary.

What a strange idea!
I think of my own name,
unchanging through the years,
like the mix of blue-gray
in my irises.

Mom says I'm named after Judy Garland.
What if they had called me Dorothy instead?
Would I have invisible red shoes
to show my heart how to find its true home?

Deep in conversation about Betty Freidan and Alan Watts,
I don't see Eddie's jealous glances,
the rage threatening to erupt.
I don't notice when he storms out,
leaving me without a way home.
The minister drives me to my tiny apartment
before he returns Gary to Elmendorf.

That night, I lie in my bed,
thinking my name should be Turtle,
the way I pull into my shell,

refusing to acknowledge the dangerous anger
behind Eddie's easy charm.

I drift into uneasy sleep,
never suspecting that by September
I will be changing my last name to Gary's.

STAR SAPPHIRE

When Gary shows up on my doorstep,
darkness frames his smiling face.
He carries a vinyl long-play record
under one arm — for me, he says.
I stifle a giggle, remembering
the gigantic watermelon
he brought last week.

Robert Goulet croons as we sprawl on the beige rug,
dining on Swanson fried chicken TV dinners.
Afterward, I offer homemade peanut butter cookies,
but he declines, tells me he has something else for me,
tugging a small box from his pocket.

His voice rolls out of an ice cave,
spewing sparks.
I barely hear his will-you-marry-me.
My *yes* realigns the cosmos,
the way the Great Alaska Earthquake
split Anchorage down the middle,
changing the landscape forever.

After Gary slips the ring on my finger,
I hold it under the bright ceiling light.
One perfect star emerges from the sky-blue stone.

That night, I call my parents collect with the good news.
They don't understand. How could they?
I realize too late — I don't know his last name!
He is just Gary to me.
I'm afraid they will come to Alaska
to take me back home, but they don't.

That ring disappeared long ago, but fifty years later, it still forms that same fiery star under our skin, whenever we stand in the light.

ALASKA HONEYMOON

I select my trousseau: a new pair of jeans,
an oversized red hooded sweatshirt,
blue flannel pajamas.
Gary crams cans of tuna,
boxes of Ritz crackers
and a bag of onions
into our suitcases.

We try to sneak away early the next morning, but too late!
Our friends have scrawled white wedding words
all over Gary's green Opel Kadett,
taped a gigantic bow to the luggage rack
and set a string of tin cans to tumble and clang.
We giggle until we hoot and snort,
finally disconnecting the noisy cans
so we don't arouse the whole apartment complex.

We meander north toward Nome in a string of days,
stopping on the way to gasp in wonder
at a family of moose in silhouette across a lake.
One day we slog along a dried-up river bed,
stalking a school of imaginary salmon
who are fighting their way upstream to spawn.
We climb hills and squint
as far as we can see,
like reflections in a series of mirrors.

Memories, like snapshots, settle in the folds of my mind.
I retrieve echoes of laughter, harmonizing in the car,
"Santa Lucia," "Three Jolly Coachmen," "Silent Night,"
returning to Anchorage on that last day of our honeymoon,
surrounded by a gentle snowfall.
Feather-light clumps drift down, cling to stubby pine,
hushed and holy in the fading light.

MARRIED LIFE

THIS IS HOW I WOULD LIKE TO DO THE DISHES

This is how I would like to do the dishes when Gary was supposed to do them, but he says he was doing watercolors instead. It is my day off and three days' worth of dishes are piled up in the sink and not orderly, but a plate, a cup, a frying pan, a glass, another plate, all with forks and spoons and knives on them and a greasy spoon in the water glass. So why don't I just pile them in the middle of the kitchen floor and turn the water on until the sink overflows and the water rises . . .

But first it would tumble down the stairwell like a beautiful waterfall until it filled that up, and then the water would rise higher and higher until all the dishes were covered with water so I could just upend the yellow dish detergent that smells like lemons and splash around to make suds. After a while I would wash the dishes with my feet, just to see what it feels like, and to see if I can still pick up a fork with my toes like I could when I was eight years old, but by then I would have to pile up all the dishes on top of the refrigerator to dry off because the countertops would be covered with water, and maybe I would have to dive down to find the dishes now, and the cat would have to find a dry place to sit because he hates to get wet, or he could learn to swim.

He could learn to do the cat-paddle, and we could do laps like in the pool, only the water would be warm like in the hot tub. Everything would either get clean or melt away like all those outdated coupons, and you couldn't see the dirty rugs anymore. Our foam beds would float and make a raft, so that we could paddle to China or maybe the Milky Way, and Carl Sagan would ask me to write about what it was like to spiral toward the center on lemon-scented bubbles.

Because he has never actually seen the Milky Way except through a telescope, maybe he would come for dinner, and maybe he would tell Gary that he is married to an extraordinary woman who experiences stars in a unique way and is able to translate those experiences so brilliantly that the entire scientific community is impressed.

But Gary, remembering how he opened the door and tumbled head over heels down the stairs in a flood of lemony water, would say . . .

"Yes, but she doesn't know how to do the dishes!"

THE MYSTERIOUS POWER OF HOUSEWORK

On the bathroom and kitchen floors,
where linoleum provides
an ideal environment for lovers,
dust-bunnies explore each other
with inquisitive noses.
Soon baby bunnies hop
on our wall-to-wall carpet
to feed on leaves and twigs
tracked in on sticky dog feet.

Without vacuum and Swiffer mop,
they will proliferate quickly,
spilling out over the windowsills
to play on our deck.

"The dish ran away with the spoon" had it right.
Those dirty dishes had triplets —
a butter knife, a fork, and this
morning's coffee cup.
After a lightning quick trip to Vegas,
the soup pot and the frying pan returned
with three dirty plates
and a bowl.

"The dishwasher again?"
Gary asks incredulously.
"Two people can't possibly generate
a full load every day."
No, but the dishes can.

A towering stack of paper bags
totter at the far end of our kitchen counter,

even though we own seventeen
canvas, reusable shopping bags.
Hangers multiply in the closet.
Four books I bought at the library book sale
turn into hundreds of paperbacks.
They sit piggyback on my nightstand,
hide under the couch, or crouch
precariously on the arm of the living
room chair.

Once, our son, Noel, after looking
around at the clutter,
suggested a cleaning lady,
but I don't need a housekeeper.
I need birth control!

THIS IS HOW YOU HANG UP THE CLOTHES

The wind floats the wet clothes
away from you.
Stiff wooden clothespins,
worn smooth under your fingers,
give off the faint smell of pine.

They arrange themselves in patterns,
white clothing, sun-bleached
dark clothing, cool in shadiness.

Always you are reaching up
sun-squinted toward heaven,
mingled with the scent of
prairie grass, fresh air,
sunshine and clean, wet clothes.

And sometimes in the middle
of an Iowa winter,
you can shake out a sheet
from the bottom of the chest
and smell that sweetness.

WALKING BEVERLY'S SCHNAUZER

Lifting one back leg out of a snowdrift,
Gretchen pees yellow ribbons in the snow.
Looking up Lowe Street,
I surprise a gigantic moon hanging low in the east.
Shimmering, insubstantial,
winter's mirage.

I snuffle along the ground,
push my nose deep into the snow,
my hands like snowplows, clearing a path ahead.
White flakes tickle my nose into sneezing.
Multiple explosions expose a small, naked doll,
a two-year-old's baby.
I seize the sleek, rubbery form
between sharp teeth,
shake my shaggy head back and forth.
Grrr! . . . Grrr!

"Drop that!" Gretchen barks.
But I am past all obedience.
The fur along my back lifts.
Red eyes reflect off slippery surfaces.
I leap backward, freeing the blue neon leash.
Carrying my baby in my mouth,
I lope up Lowe Street.
At the top of the hill,
I sit back on my haunches and howl.

The frozen doll
clatters down the icy street
and is silent.

The moon floats higher,
diminished, more substantial,
transformed into
something else.

LUCKY DOG

Beverly's schnauzer yanks the leash out of my hands,
racing across the newly mowed grass at City Park.

The gray squirrel sprints up a maple tree,
and is scolding from a high branch
when I finally catch up.

Kylie's nails scrabble on the bark,
confident that he can climb the tree.
Ruff! Ruff! Ruff!
Jaws open wide, eyes fixed
on his chattering nemesis above.

I laugh out loud. *Kylie, there's no way*
you are ever going to catch that squirrel.
Dogs can't climb trees.

At that very moment,
the squirrel loses his balance,
falls off the branch straight
into Kylie's gaping mouth.
The dog stares at me, bewildered,
squirrel dangling from either side of his muzzle.
What do I do now?

DROP IT! I bellow, and Kylie does.
Squirrel scampers out of sight in seconds
as we both stand stock still,
stunned by the impossibility of it all.

MOON

In my comic book, Donald Duck eats
green cheese from the moon,
but I think it looks more like Swiss.
Sometimes I can see a face,
mouth open in perpetual astonishment.
At other times, a giant's ice cream scoop
carves out a generous serving,
leaving a slender crescent.
Mother says it's just the earth's shadow.
Do shadows eat green cheese?

After I am married, men walk on the moon.
Now, as I gaze in wonder at its changing face,
the shifting shadows form ancient letters
in a language I knew eons ago.

Goodnight Moon is Noel's favorite bedtime story,
and "moon" becomes one of his first words.
He points to the circle on the page
and whispers the word over and over,
like an incantation.
One night when he is teething,
neither book nor lullaby can soothe his crying.
Impulsively, I wrap a blanket around him,
take him outside where waving palm leaves
gently fan the air, and a full Filipino moon
more than compensates for the lack of streetlights.
Noel whimpers softly on my shoulder
as I walk up and down the sidewalk.

I feel Noel raise his head.
His hiccuping sobs change to delighted laughter.
"Moon," he whispers, pointing to the sky.
"Moon, moon, moon," louder and louder.
He jumps up and down so hard in my arms,
I'm afraid I'll drop him.
"MOON!"

RENAL TRANSPLANT

His insults shower all of us, like the dirty puddles
spewed over pedestrians by an angry truck driver.
As nurses, we have to take turns caring for him
just to keep our tempers in check.

Devon is fourteen, but acts like a two-year-old,
fighting every procedure, wanting only to be left alone
to read his comic books.
His face and body, bloated
from failed kidneys and prednisone,
emphasize the thinness of his arms, his legs,
which are no longer able to hold him up.
As we lift him into a wheelchair,
I try not to think of a toad.

None of us want him to die,
but as the months go on,
it becomes harder and harder
to keep his frail body going.

One morning we come in to discover
that he finally got his kidney.
The abusive language continues,
but he becomes more cooperative,
anxious to get home — and away from us!

A year later, I see a handsome young man
standing outside the nurses station
holding a large bouquet of yellow roses.
I ask if I can help him find a room number.
He gives me an attractive smile,
says he is here to thank the nurses.
His eyes light up with fun,

"You don't recognize me, do you. I am Devon!"

LIFE IN CALIFORNIA

STARS

Deserted streets, shadowed in dim streetlights,
look unfamiliar where just moments before,
I had seen the Lawrence College Chapel
and thought I was almost home.
Now all the landmarks have disappeared
and dry leaves sweep the sidewalk
clean of all I once knew.
I struggle out of a tangled dream
where I am lost in the Wisconsin town
of my childhood.

I get out of bed, still disoriented
in our new house, feeling along the wall
until I find the bathroom.
Then, instead of going back
to bad dreams and darkness,
my bare feet shuffle across the living room
where I slide the dead bolt
and step out onto the deck.

Far below, the lights of Sonoma
cast a pale glow over the mountains
on the other side of the valley.
A cool wind gently ruffles my nightgown,
soothes my hot skin and fills my longing.
When I look up, I see a profusion of stars,
far more stars than I will ever need
to find my way home.

THE LANGUAGE OF OWLS

The sun vanishes behind the mountain
just as the moon appears
above the eucalyptus trees,
but I don't notice.
Nor am I aware of the oak and pine
that encircle our house turning ebony
against a pale gray sky,
like the pictures of children
in my old Sunday School books,
black sillouettes on a white page
as if we are all shadows.

The rising sound of cicadas,
punctuated by an occasional frog croaking,
slides past ears turned inward,
bouncing off the inside of my skull
like ping-pong balls in an empty room.

"Cauliflower soup for supper.
Garbage pick-up tomorrow.
Did we pay the water bill?"

If the evening mountain breezes stroke my skin
in an effort to awaken lethargic nerve endings,
I don't feel it. If Jupiter bursts into existence
close to the moon, I don't see it.
It's as if my eyes are installed backwards,
staring into a convoluted brain,
flashes of light illuminating past mistakes.

A sound so loud, I think it is coming from inside of me.
Whoo whoo! Whoo whoo! Whoo-whoo-whoo!
I look wildly around an empty deck.
Whoo whoo. Whoo whoo. Whoo-whoo-whoo.
Much fainter and coming from the woods in back of the house.
Two of them, then a male and his lover, perhaps.

I lean over the railing, scan the trees,
At the very top of the tallest pine,
perched on a dead branch, an enormous owl.
They call back and forth half a dozen times
before he unfolds wings too large to believe
and floats over treetops
through air made mysterious by their canticle.

RAKE WOMAN

Pale brown leaves collect
around the porch stairs, the stone fence,
leftovers from last fall,
reminders of two bad knees
and a stiff shoulder that locks up
when I lift the heavy rake,
souvenirs of thirty-five years
lifting hospital patients.

This morning I start an eight-week fitness class.
The dreaded treadmill leers at me
from its intimidating instrument-panel eyes,
daring me to step onto its sly tongue
that I know will toss me out on the gray carpet.
I tell our instructor I'm terrified.
Anastasia shakes her ponytail and laughs,
tells me I'll want to pay attention
to the safety information.

OK, I'm on the treadmill,
but I won't do the five minutes.
Five minutes later I am stepping down on wobbly legs.
My hands tremble, my heart quivers, but I feel alive.

I picture myself in a red cape and black tights.
By night I roam the Sonoma mountains,
howling at the moon as it rises over the misty hills.
But, by day I am Rake Woman, scraping up the layers
of dead leaves that surround my life,
swirling them into balls of kindling
before hurling them into the sun.

GRAY CAT RUNNING

After weeks hiking along the road
overlooking the Valley of the Moon,
the steep hills and thin mountain air
still force me to stop at intervals
to gasp for air, legs trembling.
That's when I see a small gray mound
in the middle of dark asphalt — road kill?

I smile in relief when the shape of a cat
unfolds itself and turns to look at me.
But then her eyes widen in fright.
She streaks up the long driveway
as if a thousand demons were after her.
Am I really that scary?

I see her every day after that,
and every day she runs from me in terror.
Am I so filled with anger at our ruined economy,
the war, at getting old, that my rage
has turned me into a monster?

On this morning's walk, I stop to catch my breath
and spot that familiar gray shape.
This time, I close my eyes and focus on the cat,

"You are so beautiful," I whisper.
    "I would never hurt you.
        Please don't run away."

When I open my eyes,
the cat is strolling toward me.

Her purr reaches me before she does,
and then catlike, she weaves in and out
between my feet, rubbing my legs with her muzzle.
Enchanted, I bend down to stroke soft electric fur,
from the top of her head to the tip of her tail.
She pushes a cold, wet nose into my hand.

When I turn around at the stop sign
at the top of the hill, the cat is gone,
but an orange sun breaks over the mountains,
suffusing the clouds with apricot light
stitching the edges in bright gold.

MAGNETIC FIELDS

Morning light filters through
pale gray fog, this moving curtain,
background for the slender fingers of green
on redwood branches outside my window.

Beyond the old stone fence,
shadow trees reach toward the sky,
defying gravity in an attempt
to touch the sun.

I feel my own light filter through
this misty landscape of language,
my words like fingers
reaching through the luminous air.

WHALE WATCHING AT SCHOOLHOUSE BEACH

The sea sparkles deep turquoise.
Far from shore a whale,
humping the surface again and again,
adds his dark reflection to pieces of sky,
the water tinged with brownish sand.

Gary and I watch the waves
from the front seat of our gold Honda Accord.
Fargo, sitting on my lap, seems more interested
in the swooping seagulls
tacking unsteadily in the cold wind.

We open the windows so we can hear
the crashing of water hitting sand,
more vibration than sound,
trembling through the floor
and the soles of my sandals,
the actual sound almost too low
for my human ears.

Huge jagged rocks catch walls of water at their peak,
sending white spray high into the air.
We wonder why these rocks aren't round
after years of pounding.
For how long has this vast expanse of water
been carving away at the California coastline?
How many generations of whales, sharks, and sea lions?
At what moment did that rough beast
slouch out of the sea onto unfamiliar land?

DRIVING TO THE CALIFORNIA COAST

We decide to go despite the rainy weather,
anticipating near empty beaches,
waves wonderfully high
as they emerge from a gunmetal sea,
crashing against dark, wet rocks,
white plumes over thirty feet in the air.

It starts out as a smudge of color,
floating over the vineyards on the left.
I think it's trying to be a rainbow.
A few minutes later, the colors pile up
to form part of an arc.

Our excitement builds as the colorful bands
extend the arc across a misty sky,
only to plunge into a bank of gray clouds.
The road turns and the rainbow disappears
among groans of disappointment.

The next turn brings oohs of delight
as bright colors reappear in a complete bow.
Two pot o' gold feet straddle the road,
skim over newly green fields.

Even though I know better, I am convinced
that we are about to pass through
this primordial portal,
leaving the rainbow far behind.
But the colorful arc skips just ahead of us,
deftly climbing hills and leaping
over the giant rocks that litter this coastal land.

I imagine our gold Accord
zooming underneath that watery prism
to the other side of the enchanted arch,
where craggy rocks speak our language
and two suns cast double seagull shadows
on the yellow sand.

ENCHANTED THURSDAY

We leave in the middle of writing my to-do list,
because the weather man says
the waves will be eighteen feet high today.

Even the sky seems a little nuts.
Three perfectly parallel cloud horns
blow wispy strands of music toward an azure ceiling.
Over the mountains, graceful ballerinas
in frothy white tutus pose en pointe.
Meanwhile, the horns morph
into filmy, transparent curtains
that vanish when we are not looking.

Gary and I leave our Honda to walk around,
so we can watch those enormous white waves
crash against rocks or on the sand,
stretching toward steep cliff walls
with flat, shining tongues.
Their thunder vibrates my skin,
pounds the bass drum of my bones.

On the other side of the cove,
the ocean generates a line of white stallions
racing toward the shore,
hooves tucked under their bellies,
sea-spray manes flying above stretched-out necks.
Hurtling onto the sand, they disappear,
hooves, heads and manes, back into the sea.

The hills between Bodega Bay and Petaluma
seem strangely altered
by shadows cast in the sinking sun,

the rough, green grass smoothed to polished jade.
I can sense something invisible hovering far above
black cattle standing silent and still
against the darkening hillside.

FOX

I look out my kitchen window
to see if the bluebirds found the whole-wheat
crumbs on our deck railing.
A small silver fox nibbles at the bird's breakfast,
bushy tail longer than his body.

"Has to be a coyote," Noel says,
but I've seen that foxy face before
staring at me from the pages of *National Geographic*.

Two days later, the fox squats
over our *Press Democrat*
at the bottom of the driveway.
I had been so sure it was a neighbor's dog
staining our morning newspaper.

We buy bird feeders and seed to replace
the cracked plate of leftover bread.
The deck visits stop, but I see him sometimes,
trotting far ahead of me on my morning walks,
and he still marks our newspaper
with a yellow dampness that penetrates
clear down to the sports section.

I think that fox is laughing at us.
I hear him sometimes in my dreams.

NIGHTMARE NUMBER TWO

In my dream, a harness
attached to a track in the ceiling
holds me suspended,
takes me from classroom to classroom.
Language is my only source of power.

I live in a plaster cast,
arms and legs enclosed,
trapped in a bizarre position,
like when I jumped off the high dive for the first time,
panic caught in my flailing limbs.

All my teachers are gathered around a table
which holds the empty cast, the harness,
aluminum track bars.
They are smiling, telling me
I don't need my fear anymore.
If I just let go and relax,
the water will naturally
carry me up to the light.

ANOTHER KIND OF RAPTURE

On the cliff overlooking Schoolhouse Beach,
separated by windshield glass,
we watch a deep azure sea spin whitecaps
into lacy embellishments that look too fragile
to produce the thunderous sounds
that tremble our bones.

Our Mini Aussie, Fargo, sitting between us,
tracks a flock of pelicans
that fly through gusts of wind
that waver the smaller seagulls.
Above the ruffled cobalt ocean,
clouds form wispy feathers,
unreadable lines of writing,
thick saucer-shaped discs.
The distant horizon pulls my eyes
toward an invisible line.

An older Toyota pulls up
and a boy jumps out of the back seat
wearing a tan and green striped shirt,
cutoffs, and worn tennis shoes.
Racing to the edge of the cliff,
he stands there a moment,
knees bent, arms outstretched.
"YES!" he screams!

Lifting his arms to the sky,
he jumps, eyes closed,
mouth in a wide open smile,
to taste the joy.

READING THE REDWOOD

I sit on my deck in the wrought-iron chair,
gazing at the hundred-foot redwood
just outside our bedroom window.
On windy nights we hear it reaching out needle arms
to scritch-scratch on the side of the house,
a giant cat wanting to come in,
or maybe a poet
writing in invisible ink on the wooden shingles.

I sink through the hard clay soil
to mingle with tangled roots of the tree.
I feel the strength of stones,
the accommodating nature of water,
the energy of earthworms, coiled and safe
beneath the cooling branches.

And below it all, a whisper,
breathing the alphabet into existence.

SONOMA COAST

So impulsive, this drive to the coast
after buying shower curtains in Santa Rosa.
Gray skies and drizzle blur the looming hills,
add shine to strange rocks
that emerge out of the earth,
the twisting roads made slick with rain.

By the time we pull up to the cliff edge
overlooking Carmet Beach, we are arguing
about whose idea it was to come out here anyway.
Wind drives thick rain against the windshield,
blocking our view of the ocean.
From the back seat Fargo whimpers,
wanting his usual walk,
but disliking the rain almost as much as we do.

When the rain stops,
Gary turns the windshield wipers on one more time.
Waves leap up like giant water spirits,
towering white froth that hangs suspended for a moment
before crashing back into itself,
sending spumes flying above the crest.

Enough energy to light up the chambers
of our overcast hearts.

HORSES

As dusk settles into stillness,
I hear their ghostly neighs
floating in the darkening air.
Here, on the hillsides above Sonoma,
horses sleep in stables beyond the trees,
out of sight, phantoms of the night.
By day, you sometimes see them out in grassy fields,
as if posing for a calendar, tossing their heads,
manes shimmering in the California sun.

One poor old horse,
dressed in an olive green blanket,
stands in his little field next to the road,
leaning a little, as if to topple over.
We are afraid that one day
he will collapse and disappear.
Serene and still, he dreams
of green meadows,
running through wild wheat,
as we zoom down the mountain.

I remember the horses of my youth,
how much they taught me, and I long to cling
to their reassuring backs one more time.
But they are all ghosts.
I need something more substantial
to carry me through this mad, accelerating world.

SEASCAPE

Oceans live inside my head.
They batter the sand and spatter rocks,
tossing luxury liners back and forth like beach balls
with arms made of water.
Sailors call her She, like their ships.
She cradles dolphins, sharks, sea lions,
sings them to sleep with a shushing lullaby.

Sometimes, when I swim
on the sandy ocean floor,
next to blind fish and darkness
the rhythms of her tides
become my breathing.

EARTHWORMS IN THE RAIN

Windy cinders swirl in the rain.
Creek runs hurly-burly down the hill, singing
tink-a-da, tink-a-da, tink-a-da to the earthworms
that slide squirmy and straight across the road.
Stretchy-long, banded in yellow,
they tremble the rough pavement
with inquisitive, touchy noses.

I am afraid to dance too wildly
around such fragile beauty,
these beguiling creatures in the morning mist,
slender jewels that survive
frigid winter rain, baking summer heat.

When I was a child, I imagined
they floated up from flooded homes,
then crawled to the asphalt plain
until the water retreated.
I would scoop them up off the sidewalk,
carrying them in cupped hands
to a place of safety under the lilac bushes,
far from heavy feet.

DOG DAYS

THE ULTIMATE CHRISTMAS GIFT

Noel's phone call catches me off guard.
"I want to surprise Dad, but is it OK with you?"
Now he stares at me, this Christmas puppy,
one eye the icy blue of a winter sky,
the other, deep brown like the polished chestnut
I kept in my pocket when I was seven.
The reality of it all leaves my mind racing.
When this puppy is fifteen, we'll be eighty-five!
Gary's look is more incredulous than pleased.
"A puppy?" he repeats over and over,
as if this incantation will make the illusion disappear.
Noel tells us his name is Fargo,
but they've been calling him Little Dog.

Our negotiations spread out over nearly a year.
He has to sleep on the floor at night,
but we allow him on the couch or in my dad's old chair.
I let him steal and guard my smelly socks
if he agrees not to chew holes in them.
Fargo takes me for morning walks to watch the sun
splash mountain clouds with peach and gold.
I lose weight and my legs get stronger.

He is smart, easily bored, so I teach him
to sit and stay, roll over and fetch.
He teaches us the benefits of an open heart.

FINDING FARGO

I notice his puppy eyes
as we stare at each other for the first time,
one blue eye and one brown
boring into my skull.
I feel a shiver of recognition,
wonder if he feels it too.

I've been searching for this dog all my life,
and now he's appeared
when I wasn't even paying attention.
I worry that our old frail bones
can't walk him enough,
that racing around our yard after invisible sheep
will never feel like real work to him.

But I can feel the truth seeping up
from the soles of my feet —
that Fargo was seeking us too,
that my hunger was never one-sided,
that my guardian angel merely waited
for this exact moment
to bring us together.

THIS MORNING

Fargo and I walk into an orange sky.
A cloud kitten curls between two hills,
ears cupped to capture the morning.
Overhead, dolphin and baby leap
out of a coral-colored sea, while farther down,
four cloud children, lined up on a bobsled,
glide silently across shadowy mountaintops.

These playful formations stir my imagination
the way this chilly sea breeze
pushes treetops into such sinuous motion
that even I feel like dancing.
I notice the way the wind sways wild wheat
that grows along the dirt road,
the sudden gust lifting my hair.
I see the light that seems to emerge from leaves
when the sun is low in the sky,
the flickering of a distant galaxy,
the luminosity when I gaze
into my dog's two-colored eyes.

When I look deep within
the big moss-covered rock
at the end of our driveway,
I sense something stirring,
ancient, patient, older than earth.

DONALD O'CONNOR

tap-dances himself into my dream,
the same way a floppy-eared dog
will thrust a cold, wet nose
into your pocket,
looking for the answers
to all his longings.

But then Donald, that sly transformer,
morphs into me!

In my aquamarine tutu,
I leap and sail across a stage
that strangely resembles my high school gym.
Thousands cheer and gasp in wonder
as I walk up the wall into a perfect back flip,
or hurl myself toward star-filled skylights.
What grace, what lightness inhabits my perfect body!
A new way to fly!

The crowd jumps up and down, screaming;
they pause to hold their breath
as I float over their heads like a blue dolphin,
turning slowly in the light of their admiration,

until the early morning sun
throws slanted lines of light across my face.

DOG DREAMS

Fargo stretches out
on the patchwork baby quilt I bought
at a garage sale for ten cents.
Even in sleep, he grows out of puppyhood,
soft muzzle elongating, sharper now,
fat puppy legs morphing into Liza Minnelli gams
that leave bruises on my thighs
when he jumps into my lap.

As our Mini Aussie dozes,
his paws twitch restlessly,
jaws quivering, almost imperceptible snuffling,
faint whine, my own head
nodding, drowsy.

Fargo herds ancestral sheep in ghostland,
chases them into circle,
turning on a penny to change direction,
nipping at recalcitrant hooves.

I feel the grassy ground
disappear beneath my paws,
the exhilaration of running.
Energizing oxygen fills my generous heart
with pride in keeping safe
all those entrusted to my care,
I circle the herd again and again,
until exhausted, I spiral
into dreamless sleep.

EVEN A MORNING WITHOUT CLOUDS

The sun, not yet up, casts a peachy glow
along the Sonoma hilltops
on the other side of the Valley of the Moon.
Such stillness, the silence
broken only by the last soft hoots of owls
somewhere among the redwoods.
Fargo sniffs the ground,
ears alert to catch any unexpected sounds,
other dog walkers perhaps, or maybe deer.
The crunching sound of my footsteps on the gravel
joins the *shush-shush* sound of the creek
as we near the little bridge,
and the last hoot of the owl fades into morning.

The first bird call pierces the air,
his song, more police whistle than psalm.
Other chirps and cries join in
and the *tat-tat-tat* of a woodpecker,
all quietness vanished with the dawn.

Just as the sun breaks above the mountains,
I spot two earthworms struggling on the dry pavement,
their glossy skins dulled by bits of dirt and sand.
I pick them up carefully and carry them,
squirming in my palm, to the side of the road
where I hope the broad leafy greens, still dewy and cool,
will shield them from the sun
and restore some moisture to their skin.

Fargo looks at me, curious.
In that instant, my chest cracks open
and I feel the enormity of it all,
the fragility of life
and the strong connections
that link us all, as close as breathing.

WAKING UP

Fargo licks my face, whimpers a little,
then dances over to the makeshift table
where we keep his leash.
He stares at me, waiting.
A walk? Yes. Good idea.
Who could resist those pleading eyes?

By six a.m., the sun has already emerged
from behind the greening hilltops.
It hangs there for a moment before vanishing
behind layers of dark gray clouds.
Not fog exactly, but a delicate mist
softens the bright greens of rosemary along the road,
darkens tall redwoods across the field
and transmutes the spring hills
into varying shades of light olive.
To the west, a three-quarter moon
hovers over the hill behind our strange, octagonal house.

Fargo, far more interested in the creek,
pulls me over to the bridge
where we watch the water
flowing over the rocks in silvery braids,
chanting its matins to an awakening world,
and to me.

REFLECTIONS

Fargo and I turn to watch the sun
peek over the Sonoma mountains.
Surprise — an identical sun
glares off the neighbor's picture window.
I wouldn't be able to tell the difference
if one of them wasn't surrounded by a house.

I remember seeing my terrified, two-year-old face
mirrored in my mother's eyeglasses,
her face too close, her mouth a straight line.
Giving me a little shake, she asked over and over,
"What did you do?"
I didn't know what I did.

My child-self, in beat up tennis shoes,
tap-dances in front of the French doors
in our old house on Franklin Street.
It's not me I see reflected in the glass squares,
but Donald O'Connor in "Singing in the Rain."

"Did you hear me?" Gary says.
"I just told you that you look beautiful."
I look into warm brown eyes,
and see that he believes this.
I manage to stammer out a thank you.

Tonight, we all sit out on the deck
to enjoy the night sky.
Fargo licks my fingers, pushes a cold wet nose
into the palm of my hand.
So clear up here.

My eyes reflect faint light
from the furthermost star,
my mind, unable to grasp
such vastness.

RETREAT

I'm beginning to regret our early morning walk.
Thick fog, falling in curtains of gray,
obscures the road ahead, changing Kenleigh Drive
into something unfamiliar.
Threatening.

The pavement feels uneven
beneath my uncertain feet,
but Fargo runs easily among
magenta thistles and wild blackberries
scattered along the side of the road.
Like a ghost, he appears and disappears
in the heavy morning mist.

On a clear morning
I can hear a car coming
from half a mile away,
but now the sound of an engine
emerges right behind us,
startling in its nearness.
Fargo lunges after a gray Ford Escort,
growling at this strange beast.
I imagine my furry companion
tangled under the wheels
and pull back sharply on the leash.

We are safe for the moment.
Fargo presses against my legs, whining a little.
I turn around and take small careful steps
back to the big moss-covered rock,
then up our long gravel driveway
where a soft light from the kitchen window
welcomes us back home.

WALKING THE KENWOOD PARK PATH

My legs, pillars of pain
after a brutal water aerobics workout,
protest the trek around the park,
but I've promised Fargo a walk today.
I tell my recalcitrant limbs the land is flat here,
not like the steep hills at home
and urge them forward.
Reluctantly, they lurch ahead,
grumbling about gray skies, the cold breeze.

Fargo races ahead to lift his leg
against the pooper-scooper sign,
gives a sigh of relief as the yellow river
bubbles to the edge of the sidewalk.
Eager to check out other doggie scents,
he prances around every bush and tree,
sniffing enthusiastically, his nose
sorting out the mix of intriguing odors.

Up ahead, the path glows purple-pink,
fallen blossoms turning the path
into a photographic negative of the yellow brick road.
We follow the fuchsia carpet into a Technicolor world,
where budding leaves turn twiggy branches spring green.
A window in the sky flashes sapphire.
The little creek, rushing and noisy last week,
lies grassy and calm — murmur of shallow waters —
and from a cluster of redwoods behind the Kenwood church,
the soft *whoo-whoo* of owls floats ghostlike overhead.

Halfway around the park, I sit on a bench
to admire the 150-year-old oak
which stands graceful, gnarled,
offering new pale leaves to the sky.
Ten years ago they were going to cut it down
because it was dying,
but now the Oak Restoration Project
protects the venerable tree.
Fargo rolls over and over on the cool green grass,
tongue lolling, eyes closed in ecstasy.

In a childhood memory,
I am racing headlong over the sand
towards Lake Michigan.
Freezing water splashes everywhere
as I throw myself, half screaming,
half laughing into the icy waves.
My legs kick vigorously,
propelling my dog-paddle
out to the first sandbar.

Fargo sits up to stare through me
as if I've gone somewhere else.
I can almost recall Fargo back then,
an imaginary companion swimming beside me
in those cold waters of my youth.

I look down at my gray tennis shoes with pink laces.
My legs, happy to be sitting down again, relax,
as I remember tap-dancing in front of our old French doors
when I was ten, reflections of legs
lifting me off the polished oak floor.

IN MEMORIUM

FOR JOYCE

You weave in and out of my dreams all night long.
We sit in our spacious room at the Seal Rock Inn,
happy, because this room has four single beds,
a chance to split the cost four ways instead of three.
Through the window, a cerulean sea beckons.

The glass-domed train pulls itself up the high trestle.
I am pointing toward Mt. McKinley,
or Denali, as it is called here.
Beneath the cloud-shrouded peak, moose graze,
glancing at our train with shy brown eyes.
You stare, entranced, mouth slightly open.
I knew you would love Alaska's beauty as much as I did.
You laugh and say we should plan
to climb Denali next summer.

Both of us, slightly out of breath,
stop at a scenic bridge along Lake Shore Drive.
A rosy glow over Lake Michigan's horizon
foretells the coming sunrise.
Seagulls circling the waves, emit raucous cries.
You tell me we won't really meet for another forty-five years.

Now the sun is peeking over the Sonoma mountains.
We sit on my deck, sipping coffee
as a long drift of cloud turns a rosy violet,
soft peachy-pink, and finally bright gold,
all colors in your artist's palette.

But no, we are sitting in a summer garden,
filled with pink and gold roses and fragrant lilac.

An iridescent hummingbird darts from flower to flower,
then hovers, as you cup capable hands
around the tiny vibrating body.
You turn to me with a wide smile
just before you disappear into morning.

I didn't know you had come to say good-bye.

THE PURPLE HAT

"Nice hat!"
Rudy Wilson hollers from his car,
gesturing toward his own head.
I smile, wave back, but inside,
I distrust all compliments.
My mother would have ridiculed this hat,
purple and big, framing my round face,
Purple petunias bob at the brim,
poking fun at me from the bedroom mirror,
an Aunt Hulda hat for sure.

She wore hats to church
or when we went to town for mint chip ice cream,
but when she worked in the garden,
she put on the old straw hat
with binder twine to tie it on.

"Don't forget me," she pleads
over and over again
when I go to see her for the last time.
Despite my reassurances,
she has Uncle Paul find a delicate teacup
and saucer set made in England,
and supervises while he wraps the pieces in tissue paper
and packs them in a cardboard box.
I've never unpacked those memories,
but one of these days I will take them out
and have a cup of tea just for her.

Both legs are amputated at the hip,
but her skin is as unlined and fresh
as a cool breeze off Baileys Harbor,

hair thin on top like mine is getting.
Doesn't she realize
I have a whole room full of memories?

She knows she is going to die.
I shrivel up inside like a used tea bag,
but her blue eyes are clear,
her arms filled with hugs
I no longer reach up for.
I lean over now,
feeling smothered and pleased at the same time,
just like I always did.

"Now when you see the teacups
you will think of me."

"I will never forget you,"
I whisper one last time.
How could I ever forget Aunt Hulda?
I see her face every time
I look in the mirror.

UNCLE PAUL

"Uncle Paul died last Saturday . . . bad stroke." My sister's voice sounds flat over the phone. I say something appropriate, make small talk, compare our recent snowstorms, but in my mind, I am back at Aunt Hulda and Uncle Paul's farm and it is summer.

Uncle Paul takes his pipe out of his mouth to talk to me. "How would you like to get the cows?"

"Me? You want me to go by myself?" I am ten, and no one thinks I can do things.

"Sure — it's easy. Take Pal with you. He can round 'em up. You'll find them over in the Old North Pasture."

His voice, with its Norwegian lilt, reassures me, as does his easy smile, his laughing blue eyes. He takes off his cap to wipe his face on the sleeve of his denim shirt. His sandy-red hair springs up, wild in the rough wind that scours the rocky Door County Peninsula.

I walk down the dirt road, feeling very important. Pal limps by my side, holding his back foot up. He's a good farm dog despite the old injury. The white ruff of his coat glints in the late afternoon sun. I am wondering where the Old North Pasture is, and aren't there about twenty cows — all bigger than me?

"Watch out for Daisy," Uncle Paul hollers after me. "She likes to start fights, but Pal can handle it."

The sun hangs huge and watery over the red tinted road. Pal turns right and I follow. A few minutes later I see the gate and the cows, gathered and mooing. I open the gate and Pal races around in back of the slow moving beasts, urging them through with a woof, an occasional nip, dodging the well-aimed kick. On the road, he keeps them walking single file, like well-behaved school children. Back at the barn, Uncle Paul smiles — my own grin threatening to split my face in half.

The telephone receiver hums. When did my sister hang up? All at once, I understand how one good farm dog can be worth more than twenty city kids, and how one Uncle Paul changed the direction of my life.

GHOST WHISTLE

No matter where I was in the city block
that spawned us neighborhood children,
I could hear my mother calling me home
with her unique whistle,
one long note followed by another,
an interval of a third down.
Even if I was in my favorite hiding tree,
I left right away, not wanting to risk
losing the privilege of running free
through people's backyards,
playing hide-and-go-seek or tag
from after supper until dusk.
Other mothers just called out a name,
but Mom always whistled me home.

After she died, I heard Mother's whistle in unexpected places.
I might be hanging up wet sheets in my backyard,
picking out the reddest apples at Albertson's,
or thumbing through an Agatha Christie at the library.
The clear and penetrating sound
always left me with an overwhelming desire
to return to a home that didn't exist anymore.

One day she appeared right in front of me in a wheat field,
on the other side of a barbed wire fence,
looking just like Mom, but more contented.
She smiled at me. "I just wanted to let you know
that I am happy," she said, and vanished.

I never heard that whistle again,
but maybe, when it's my time to leave this planet
I will hear it calling me home one last time.

HOSPICE

I enter the bedroom and sit
on the folding chair at the side of the bed.
My father's hands, shaped so much like my own,
lie folded across his stomach.
I take his hand and hold it,
the way he once held mine
when we were crossing a busy street.

"It's me, Judy," I whisper in his ear,
but he is already too far away.

Out of the blue, he laughs,
his eyes open and clear,
staring somewhere beyond the beige wall.

"Wait up, Walter," he calls out.
"Do you see your brother?" I ask.
"Yeah, he's clear across the field,
I'll have to run like crazy to catch up."

Later, my skeptical sister will say
it was just the morphine talking,
but I saw the figure of a child,
jumping up and down in excitement,
on the other side of a field where cows grazed,
a silhouette against the setting sun.
I could feel what it was like
to race over a field so fast
that my feet seemed to float
over the rough, grassy earth.

GONE

When I was three and Jean was ten
we went with older cousins
to see *Gone With The Wind.*
After the movie, we tumbled
out of the darkened theater to a darker outside.
I was frightened by the abrupt change
from make-believe to reality.

Jean carried me all the way home
my legs wrapped around her waist,
arms around her neck, monkey-style.
I peered over her shoulder
at streetlights casting long shadows,
noisy trolley cars rattling
in the distance.

It was years before I realized
that I never watched Milwaukee burn,
and my best friend never died
after falling off a horse.

When I was sixty-eight and Jean was seventy-five,
I went with her children to the hospital
to watch her take that last breath.
I am frightened by this abrupt change in reality.
When will I realize I can't pick up the phone
or send her the latest mystery novel?

I imagine her ashes swirling over the Fox River,
gone with the wind.

GUARDIAN ANGEL

She appears whenever I am afraid,
not like my clumsy animals
made of Play-Doh,
but carved from light,
with a suggestion
of wings.

Although I can walk right through her,
I feel her hand holding mine,
leading me away from bullies
who hide stones in snowballs.
At night she stands at the foot of my bed,
keeps monsters from grabbing my toes.

After I can't see her anymore,
she whispers in my ear,
so softly I'm not sure I hear her.
Looking back through the years,
I see how she nudges me along the path,
making sure we adopt the child
already meant to be our son,
keeping me safe through earthquakes,
hurricanes, fat bolts of lightning.

When it is my time
to fall through the fabric of life,
I hope she is there to catch me,
and carry me to the rapture of light.

ABOUT THE AUTHOR

Judy Liese grew up in Wisconsin and began writing poems as soon as she learned to print in block letters in her Big Chief writing pad. As a child, she wrote poems to entertain her friends and family. After graduating from Appleton Senior High School, she studied to be an R.N. at Columbia Hospital School of Nursing in Milwaukee, Wisconsin. After earning her R.N. degree, she accepted a job as a psychiatric nurse in Anchorage, Alaska, where she survived the 1964 earthquake and got married. For many years she worked as a nurse and wrote poetry, taking writing classes when she could. In her fifties, she earned a B.A. in Literature and a Master's Degree in English and Creative Writing from Maharishi International University in Fairfield, Iowa. Retired now, Judy and Gary, her husband of fifty years, live in Northern California to be close to their son. She has poems published in *Lyrical Iowa*, as well as in several anthologies.

This is her first full-length book of poems.

Printed in The United States of America

www.ingramcontent.com/pod-product-compliance
Lightning Source LLC
Chambersburg PA
CBHW022011090426

42741CB00007B/982